W9-BXX-834

Rainy Days

By Jennifer S. Burke

Welcome Books

Children's Press
A Division of Grolier Publishing
New York / London / Hong Kong / Sydney
Danbury, Connecticut

Photo Credits: Cover and all photos by Maura Boruchow

Contributing Editor: Mark Beyer
Book Design: MaryJane Wojciechowski

Visit Children's Press on the Internet at:
http://publishing.grolier.com

Cataloging-in-Publication Data

Burke, Jennifer S.
    Rainy days / by Jennifer S. Burke.
      p. cm. — (Weather report)
    Includes bibliographical references and index.
    Summary: A young girl describes her activities on a
rainy day.
    ISBN 0-516-23120-0 (lib. bdg.) — ISBN 0-516-23045-X (pbk.)
    1. Rain and rainfall—Juvenile literature [1. Rain
and rainfall] 1. Title. II. Series.
      2000
    551.57—dc21

Copyright © 2000 by Rosen Book Works, Inc.
All rights reserved. Published simultaneously in Canada.
Printed in the United States of America.
        3 4 5 6 7 8 9 10 R 05 04 03 02

Contents

Today it is raining.

The sky is gray.

Rainy days are not very bright outside.

Even on rainy days, I go outside.

7

I wear my **raincoat** outside.

I also wear my rubber boots.

The **rain** falls on my coat.

9

I like to reach out my hand and feel the rain.

The raindrops splash against my **palm**.

Rain makes my hand all wet.

In the car, I look out the window.

The raindrops slide down the window.

My mom turns on the **wipers**.

They wipe away the rain.

Now she can see clearly.

We go shopping at the **mall**.

My mother buys a new **umbrella**.

When we get home, it is still raining.

I like to play with puzzles on rainy days.

19

Sometimes after it rains, the sun comes out.

All the green leaves and bushes are bright.

21

New Words

mall (**mawl**) an indoor place with many
stores

palm (**polm**) the inside of your hand

rain (**rayn**) water that falls from the sky

rainy (**ray**-nee) when rain falls

raincoat (**rayn**-coht) a plastic or rubber
coat that keeps you dry

umbrella (um-**brel**-luh) a thing held over
your head to cover you from the rain

wipers (**wy**-perz) rubber arms that wipe
away water by moving back and forth

To Find Out More

Books

Can it Rain Cats and Dogs: Questions and Answers About Weather
By Melvin Berger, Gilda Berger and Robert Sullivan
Scholastic

Down Comes the Rain
By Franklyn M. Branley and James G. Hale
HarperCollins Publishers

In the Rain With Baby Duck
By Amy Hest and Jill Barton
Candlewick Press

The Rain
By Michael Laser and Jeffrey Greene
Simon & Schuster

Web Site
Weather Gone Wild
http://tqjunior.advanced.org/5818
At this site you will learn about weather and why it rains.

Index

About the Author

Jennifer S. Burke is a teacher and a writer living in New York City. She holds a master's degree in reading education from Queens College, New York.

Reading Consultants

Kris Flynn, Coordinator, Small School District Literacy, The San Diego County Office of Education

Shelly Forys, Certified Reading Recovery Specialist, W.J. Zahnow Elementary School, Waterloo, IL

Peggy McNamara, Professor, Bank Street College of Education, Reading and Literacy Program